Williamson Publishing W Charlotte, Vermont

Almost-Instant Scrapbooks

Laura Check

Illustrations by Betsy Day

Quick Starts for Kids!®

Library of Congress Cataloging-in-Publication Data

Check, Laura, 1958-
    Almost-instant scrapbooks / Laura Check ; illustrations by Betsy Day.
        p. cm. -- (Quick starts for kids!)
    Includes index.
    Summary: Provides instructions for creating various types of scrapbooks with information about collecting and preserving materials, weeding and labeling, and designing the pages and cover.
        ISBN 1-885593-90-2
    1. Photograph albums--Juvenile literature. 2. Scrapbooks--Juvenile literature. [1. Scrapbooks. 2. Handicraft.] I. Day, Betsy, ill. II.Title. III. Series.

TR465.C37283 2003
745.593--dc21
                                                              2003043097

Dedication

To my sisters and brother,
Nancy, Jane & Frank,
for always being there for me.
I love you very much!

Quick Starts for Kids!® series editor: **Susan Williamson**
Interior design: **Dana Pierson**
Illustrations: **Betsy Day**
Cover design and illustration: **Sarah Rakitin**
Technical illustrations on page 31: **Sarah Rakitin**
Printing: **Capital City Press**

Williamson Publishing Co.
P.O. Box 185
Charlotte, VT 05445
(800) 234-8791

Manufactured in the United States of America

10 9 8 7 6 5 4 3 2 1

Kids Can!®, *Little Hands*®, *Quick Starts for Kids!*®, *Kaleidoscope Kids*®, and *Tales Alive!*® are registered trademarks of Williamson Publishing.

Good Times™, *Quick Starts Tips!*™, and *You Can Do It!*™ are trademarks of Williamson Publishing.

Also by Laura Check

The Kids' Guide to Making
SCRAPBOOKS & PHOTO ALBUMS!
How to Collect, Design, Assemble, Decorate

Little Hands®
PAPER PLATE CRAFTS
Creative Art Fun for 3- to 7-Year-Olds

Contents

Way-Cool Collections — Your Way!

Welcome to the world of scrapbooking! I've been cutting, pasting, and arranging my favorite things in scrapbooks for more than 30 years. And now my children make scrapbooks right along with me. My first scrapbook was all about horses. I also have scrapbooks for my stamp collection and one about each summer. I love saving things that remind me of special people and places.

And now scrapbooking is so popular that there are specialty stores everywhere filled with the coolest scrapbooking tools and supplies I could ever dream of!

But you don't need much to get started making your own awesome scrapbooks. Using just a few basic techniques and supplies, I'll show you how to organize, sort, and put together "almost-instant" scrapbooks that will be just right for you and your interests. Plus, you'll learn to design one-of-a-kind covers of your own.

So gather your gear, and let's get started designing scrapbooks *your way!*

Laura Check

A Quick Starts® Guide to Scrapbooking

Whether you're working on your very first scrapbook or you're looking for new ideas, this is the place to begin. Here's a quick guide to what you'll need to get started, plus some basic tips and techniques for assembling and displaying all sorts of stuff.

Keep It Safe

As you make your scrapbooks, use good crafting sense.

- Ask for permission and adult help before cutting with sharp scissors or paper cutters.
- Work on thick layers of old newspaper.
- Wear old shirts or smocks when painting or printing.
- Store your tools and supplies where they will be safe and out of the way.
- Always keep small objects and sharp tools away from all young children (remember that they can reach what is on the edge of the table).

Supplies to buy, make & collect

You already have the most important tools you need to make a scrapbook: your imagination and creativity!

Combine that with a few basic supplies — paper, scissors, a ruler, glue, pens, an album (store-bought or one of your own design), and your favorite things to put inside — and you're ready to get started.

If you visit craft stores, you'll find all sorts of scrapbooking materials and tools that you can use to decorate your pages. You may want to add to your supplies a little at a time as you try the ideas in the pages that follow. No specialty tools and materials on hand? No problem! Make your own printed and decorated papers, fancy cut edges, templates, stickers, stamps, and pockets using items you have around your house.

Handy Items to Get You Started

Die cuts: Cutout shapes to glue onto your pages, made from cardboard or fabric

Edgers: Decorative cutting scissors that create fancy edges

Glues: Glue sticks, glue pens, and craft glues. See page 10 for tips on gluing.

Mounting tapes, dots, and corners: To attach items onto your pages. See page 11 for a variety of mounting materials.

Papers: Card stock and decorative papers in all colors and designs; computer paper; poster board. See page 9 for more.

Pens, pencils, markers: Fine-point, medium, and brush tips; permanent markers; gel-ink and opaque pens; a blue photo-marking pencil for labeling photos

Protective sleeves and containers: Clear plastic sleeves and trays; pockets for photos and collections

Punches: Use a *regular hole punch* for binding pages. *Fancy hole punches* in different shapes make decorative edges, and the "punch confetti" can be used as stencils or decorations.

Rubber stamps: Designs and lettering to use with paint or inks

Rulers: To measure, and to keep edges straight and corners square as you cut card stock, poster board, and other papers or fabric. *Decorative rulers* have fancy shaped edges.

Scissors: To cut out shapes, letters, mats, pages, and fabric. Use *craft scissors* for paper, *fabric scissors* for felt or fabric.

Stencils and templates: To trace shapes and letters

Stickers: Self-sticking designs and letters

Quick Starts Tips!™

Start a craft box for year-round fun! If scrapbooking is your thing, then a craft box is a great idea. In the mood to work on a scrapbook? Just pull out the box with all the things you want to use. I like to keep several craft boxes: one for my decorations, scraps, and trims; and another for tools, glue, pencils, and markers. Stencils, stamps, plastic sleeves, and papers are stored in separate plastic bags in a third box. Plus, I have a file box (page 23) of photos and collectibles. What's going to be in your craft boxes?

The Paper Chase

Card stock, computer paper, decorative papers — what's the diff? And what's best for scrapbook pages? Different types of paper have different weights, or thicknesses. Think about how you'll be using the paper and then decide what type will work best. Here are my favorites:

Card stock is a heavy, stiff paper you can use for making the inside pages of your scrapbook (the same stuff that's used to make cards!). It's stiffer than construction paper, so it holds photos and paper items nice and flat. Card stock usually comes in 8½" x 11" (21 x 27.5 cm) sheets; for extra-easy scrapbook assembly, make your covers ¼" (5 mm) larger than the precut card stock on all sides. You can buy it in plain white or in colors.

Computer paper is lightweight, and it comes in the usual white as well as an assortment of wonderful colors. It's good for mat frames, message balloons, and die cuts.

Decorative papers are sold by the sheet and in packages at craft stores. This paper is a bit heavier than computer and gel-ink papers. I use it for all sorts of scrap-booking projects — mat frames, die cuts, borders, and decorative glued designs.

Gel-ink paper is dark — great for writing on with gel-ink (opaque) pens. You can buy it in black or in colors. I use it to make frames and decorations for my pages.

Poster board is slightly heavier than card stock and usually can be bought in 11" x 14" (27.5 x 35 cm) or 22" x 28" (55 x 70 cm) sheets. It's great for making scrapbook covers.

Self-stick note papers (such as Post-it notes) are great for labeling items or events, or for writing captions in your scrapbook.

Glue & Other "Stickum" Clues

A quick look at what's out there (so you won't get "stuck" with the wrong one).

Glue sticks. My favorite! Very easy to use, no mess involved, the glue dries quickly, and they come in various sizes. Some brands have a more permanent bond than others. Great for photos and lightweight papers.

Glue pens. Easy to use, no mess involved, and they dry quickly. The various sizes of tips are ideal for hard-to-reach areas.

Glues. White liquid craft glues (like Elmer's) and *tacky glues* (all-purpose glues with an extra-strong bond) dry clear, but they take a little longer to dry than a glue stick. These work well for heavier items, such as paper pockets, brochures, postcards, and ticket stubs.

Quick Starts Tips!™

Lick-It-Later Sticker Gum. Make your own sticker gum, to use right away or in the future! All you need is 1 tablespoon (15 ml) flavored gelatin mix and 2 tablespoons (30 ml) boiling water. Pour the gelatin into a heat-proof container. Ask an adult to add the boiling water. Stir with a fork until the gelatin is dissolved. Then just brush the sticker gum on the back of artwork, paper shapes, or pictures from magazines and let dry. Later, make your sticker stick by just licking or wetting the back. Or, if you're really anxious to get those scrapbooks going, you can brush the gum on the back of your "sticker" and place it on your page right away!

When the gum in your container sets into a hard gelatin, simply set the container in a pan of hot water to turn it back to a liquid, and get stickin'!

No blobs allowed! One of the keys to making a great-looking scrapbook is to get the gluing right. That means no bumps or wrinkles! When gluing fabric or paper to another surface, place dots (not big blobs) of glue over the surface that's being covered.

Then, even out the dots with your fingers. Place the item you want to add on top of the glued surface, and press out any air bubbles with a Popsicle stick, working from the center out. For an extra-smooth look, use a glue stick or double-sided mounting tape.

Mounting materials. No mess and easy to use. Double-sided "stickies" come in dots, squares, and tape. Just stick them to the back of your photos or papers and then stick the items onto the page. You'll find them with photo or craft supplies. Or, try adhesive spray or mounting adhesive.

Mounting corners. No mess, easy to use, and they let you lift photos or papers in and out. You can buy mounting corners in colors, clear, or plain black. Some are self-stick; others need to be moistened.

Pop-ups! Easy and fun to use. These little adhesive foam dots make the items on your pages really stand out. Just stick them to the backs of photos or cutout designs to go 3-D.

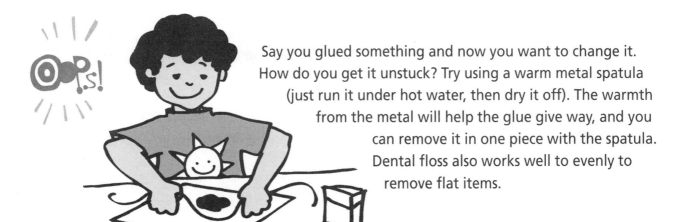

Say you glued something and now you want to change it. How do you get it unstuck? Try using a warm metal spatula (just run it under hot water, then dry it off). The warmth from the metal will help the glue give way, and you can remove it in one piece with the spatula. Dental floss also works well to evenly to remove flat items.

Stuff You Can Collect

cardboard boxes • cards (used) from holidays and special occasions • cereal-box cardboard • clothespins • colored chalk • computer paper • construction paper • cookie cutters • crayons • doilies • erasers • fabric scraps • markers • pencil erasers • pens and colored pencils • pinecones, pine needles, bark, leaves, shells, and other nature items • plastic lids (to make stencil cutouts) • ribbons • shoelaces • sponges • straws • string and twine • tempera paints • vegetables and fruits (for printing textures)

Other Supplies

binder rings or old binders • craft foam • paper fasteners • self-stick reinforcement circles and labels • tracing paper • zip-locking bags

Archival Alert

You're sure to come across the labels "acid free," "PVC free," "lignin free," or "archival safe" if you shop for papers, plastics, decorations, and glues for scrapbooks. What do these terms mean? Simply that there are no chemicals or materials used in making these products that might harm your collections, causing them to turn brown or age (a problem with many older albums). So, if you're buying scrapbooking materials, it's good to look for those labels. But don't let that stop you from using homemade supplies. Check out the basic supplies and tips (pages 7–12) for ways to show off and preserve your collections safely.

A note of warning: Beware of magnetic albums (the kind with self-stick boards behind clear plastic sheets). Although they're easy to use, these album pages are known for turning brown with age (plus, they lose their stickiness so your stuff falls out). Over time, the acids used in making the adhesive and the plastic pages break down — and may eventually damage your collections.

Mounting options

Three ways to keep your collections special for a long, long time!

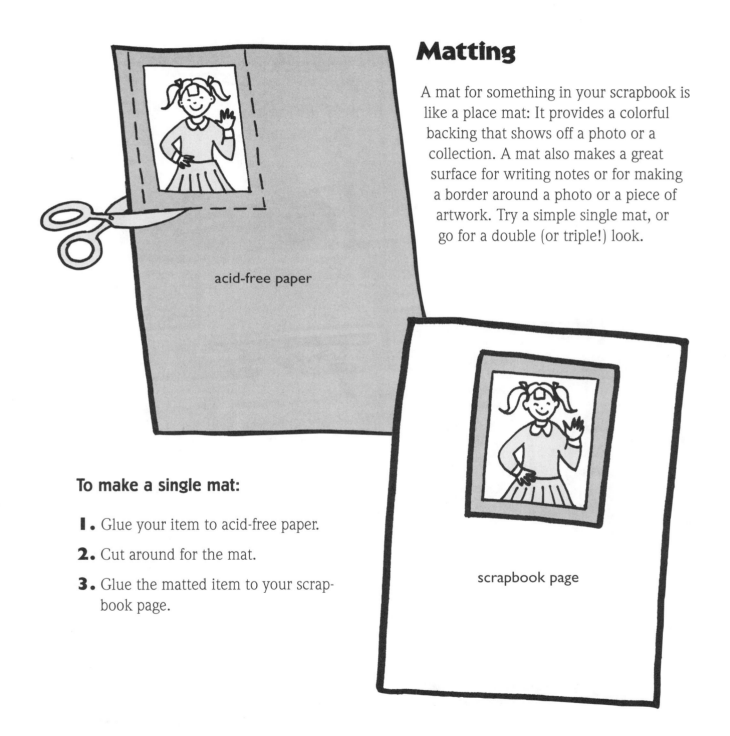

acid-free paper

scrapbook page

Matting

A mat for something in your scrapbook is like a place mat: It provides a colorful backing that shows off a photo or a collection. A mat also makes a great surface for writing notes or for making a border around a photo or a piece of artwork. Try a simple single mat, or go for a double (or triple!) look.

To make a single mat:

1. Glue your item to acid-free paper.

2. Cut around for the mat.

3. Glue the matted item to your scrapbook page.

To make a double mat:

1. Make a single mat.

2. Mark and cut a slightly larger piece of another paper to glue behind the first mat.

3. Glue the matted item to your scrapbook page.

PHOTO ON SINGLE MAT

BASEBALL CARD ON DOUBLE MAT

first mat

second mat

"Window" Treatments

Laminating (sealing items in plastic) is a great way to fully
enclose pressed flowers, newspaper clippings, pictures, cards,
tags, and other flat items. Laminating is permanent; once an
item has been sealed, it can't be removed from the plastic.
I like to laminate items with the instant self-sealing sheets
available in craft stores, and then glue displays onto a mat or
place them in a pocket or envelope inside my scrapbooks.

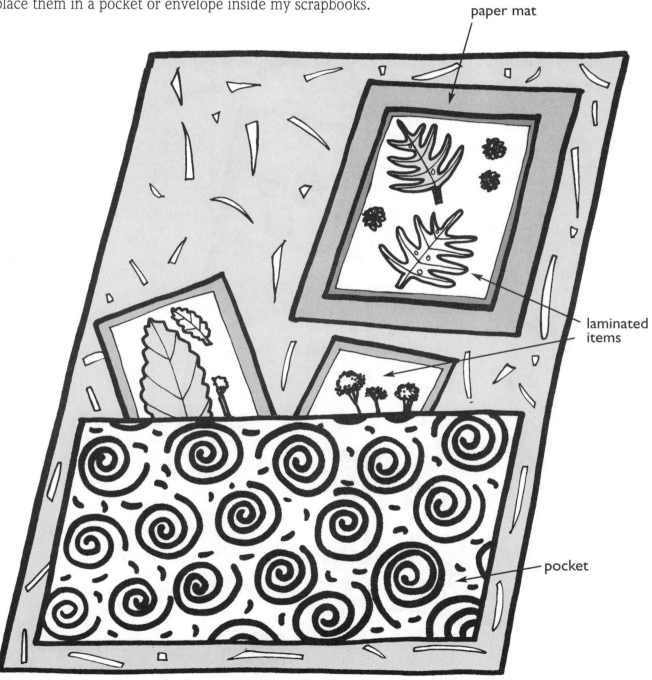

paper mat

laminated
items

pocket

Easy Sleeves and Pockets

No, we're not talking about clothing here! These are some ways to protect and hold your collections. You can get 3-D trays with snap-and-close lids to store small but bulky items like shells and pinecones. You can also buy all sorts of plastic photo pages, page protectors, pockets, and sleeves to hold your finished pages or items and protect them from dirt and fingerprints. When shopping for these plastic protectors, look for the *Mylar* types, which are safer than the PVC (polyvinyl chloride) plastics (page 12).

Use paper and stickers to make colorful pockets for ticket stubs, photos, and other souvenirs. Even a plain envelope will work fine.

large sleeves

sticker collection in a sleeve

small plastic pockets

To make a simple pocket:

Cut a shape out of decorative paper and tape or glue it to the scrapbook page on three sides, leaving the top open. For three pocket templates, see pages 58–60.

To make a two-sided pocket:

Cut decorative paper into two identical shapes (or fold in half) and glue the sides and bottom together, leaving the top open. Glue the pocket to your scrapbook page.

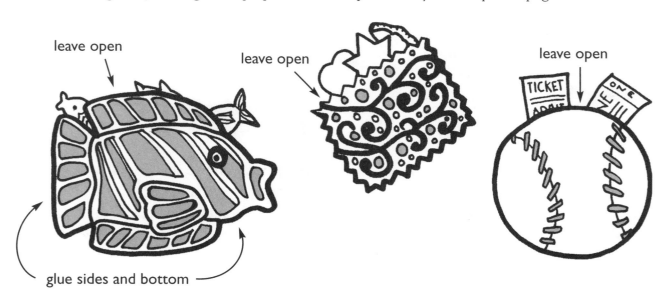

To make a gift envelope:

Trace the template on page 61 onto decorative paper (or waxed paper if you want to see what's inside) and cut and fold it together. Punch holes for a ribbon to tie closed. This is also a great way to sort and store stamps, photos, ribbons, and other small collectibles.

punch holes

Quick Starts Tips!™

To add ribbon or yarn, punch two small holes in each front flap (you can add reinforcement circles for extra strength). Thread ribbon through both holes in the bottom flap so both ends are on the outside. Then, fold down the top and thread the ribbon ends through both holes to tie.

Pocket the extras. It can be tough to decide just what to put into your scrapbooks. There's so much to choose from! Rather than agonizing over what won't fit, be creative. Pick out what will work best to tell the story about the event, and then add a full- or half-page pocket to store the extras in your scrapbook.

(see page 59 for heart pocket template)

Collecting & Sorting Your Stuff

Don't quite know where to begin? Follow these steps — one, two, three!

Step 1: Gather your stuff

Your scrapbook can include any item that means something to YOU. One word includes it all: *memorabilia*. It's everything you collect and save to remind yourself of special occasions and events in your life. Most anything can be included in a scrapbook as long as it's smaller than a shoe box. (Even then, you can include it: Photograph it and put the photo in your scrapbook!)

Maybe you're one of those kids who has mountains of memorabilia. Your challenge will be to pick and choose! If, on the other hand, your "memory pile" is so scattered about that you don't know what you have, this is the time to collect it. Don't worry if your pile is small — it's probably perfect for an "almost-instant" scrapbook.

Things to Include:

Collections: Feathers, shells, leaves, twigs, bark, flowers, pinecones, pebbles — even sand from the beach! Or, cards, beads — whatever you want to save.

Family "keepsakes": Old fabrics, buttons or pins, a special letter, family recipes

Photos: "A picture's worth a thousand words!"

School stuff: ID cards, art projects, reports, class schedules

Scouts and clubs: Sashes with badges and pins, cool info, newspaper clippings

Souvenirs: Maps, postcards, ticket stubs, hotel stationery, brochures, business cards, postage stamps, foreign coins and currency

Special occasions: Invitations, name tags, wrapping papers, cards, party favors, gift bags

Sporting events: Programs, ticket stubs, autographs, game schedules, certificates

Quick Starts Tips!™

Spread it out! Find a good area to work where you can spread out all of your stuff, but where it won't be in the way. A card table in your room or another out-of-the-way place is ideal. Then you don't have to pick it up each time you want to dig in again.

Step 2: Sort, sort, sort!

Now that you've gathered your stuff, are you asking yourself, "How in the world am I going to get all this in one little book?" Well, for starters, it doesn't all have to fit in one scrapbook. (After all, your whole life didn't happen all at once, so why should you cram all your memories into one book?) Start small and simple. And sort … and then sort some more!

Choose a sorting system that makes sense for you.

Sort by Subject:

This is a good choice for scrapbooks about sports, pets, community groups, clubs, religious groups, Scouts, hiking and camping trips, and vacations. Keep sorting into smaller groupings until you end up with manageable piles.

(see page 62 for portfolio template)

Sort by Year:

A *chronological* (year-by-year) method works well for family, friends, or school scrapbooks. Sort a year, month by month, or sort each year into smaller subject categories that are meaningful to you, such as holidays, birthdays, sports, and vacations.

Jot It Down, Now!

Even though you think you'll never forget, you'll be surprised at how quickly the details and dates of photos and ticket stubs fade from your memory. Use a special blue photo-marking pencil (available from photography or craft stores) or sticky tabs on the back of photos to record the info. Or, number the photos on the back and write the names and dates by the photo number on a separate piece of paper. Don't use a ballpoint pen or permanent marker — the writing may dent or "bleed" through the image.

Step 3: Weed & label

Now that you have your stuff organized, take a closer look at what you've got. Do you have lots of duplicate photos or too many quartz stones? Pull out any blurry, too-dark, or too-light shots or extra items. Put duplicates or not-so-great items in an envelope marked "Extras."

You can even make a portfolio-sized envelope for a custom fit (see template, page 62) Then, store what you want to use in an ABC File Box (see below). That way, you'll have everything you want to include in your scrapbook organized and ready to go, but safe until you need it!

Make an ABC File Box

ABC Files Boxes make it easy to sort through piles of photos and other small papers. You can buy one specifically for photographs, but it's less expensive and more fun to make your own using an old shoe box covered with decorative paper. Add poster-board or construction-paper tabs for each letter or for separate categories. File each photo or paper under the appropriate heading.

Making Almost-Instant Scrapbooks

Almost-instant scrapbooks are a perfect size for recording a single event or for giving as a gift. Imagine how pleased your grandparents (or a favorite aunt or uncle) would be if you sent them a scrapbook of things you collected and did during a visit! Those special memories are what make scrapbooks such treasures. Don't worry if you don't have a ton of stuff. Just make the size and shape scrapbook you want, and stop when you're done.
There's no set length — it's up to you!

To get started, here are eight scrapbook designs, with variations. Pick and choose ideas you like, and add new ideas of your own. Then insert your one-of-a-kind mementos and photographs. The results are sure to be awesome!

Photo or Art Folder

Make a folder into a work of art! These ready-made folders are easy to use and can pack in plenty of pages, too.

Materials

- *General supplies:* pencil, hole punch, glue stick
- *Decorating supplies:* paints, pens, permanent markers, stickers, decorative papers
- Clasp folder
- Card stock
- Artwork or photos

Let's do it!

1. Open the folder and mark the hole placements on the card stock.
2. Punch holes in as many pages as you need. Assemble the scrapbook.
3. Decorate the cover and the inside pages.

sketches on card stock

punch holes

Easy Loose-Ring Binder

This expandable loose-ring binder is great for small but bulky collections. Place the items in zip-locking bags, and label each bag with details of what's inside. Add photos and notes on card-stock pages.

Materials

- *General supplies:* pencil, ruler, scissors, hole punch, glue stick
- *Decorating supplies:* decorative paper, pens, permanent markers, stickers
- Poster board
- Zip-locking bags
- Card stock
- Self-stick labels
- Binder rings

Quick Starts Tips!™

Snack pack. At craft stores, you can purchase "project paks" containing rings and bags, or you can buy the rings separately and punch holes in snack-size zip-locking bags. Or, use rings with large sleeves that already have punched holes (page 16).

Let's do it!

1. Cut the poster board for the front and back covers about $\frac{1}{4}$" (5 mm) taller and wider than the bags. For pages, cut card stock the same size as the bags.

2. Punch holes for the rings $\frac{1}{2}$" (1 cm) in from the left-hand edge of the covers, the pages and the nonzip side of the zip-locking bags. Add selfstick reinforcement circles if desired.

3. Decorate the front cover.

4. Fill the bags with your collections. Label each bag with a self-stick label, using a permanent marker. Assemble the book.

$\frac{1}{2}$"

Rings & Binders

Sturdy store-bought O-ring binders open and close to let you remove or add pages or photo sleeves. The binder can hold mounted bulky items, too. Most three-ring binders you can buy hold $8\frac{1}{2}$" x 11" (21 x 27.5 cm) pages, but they also come in smaller and larger sizes.

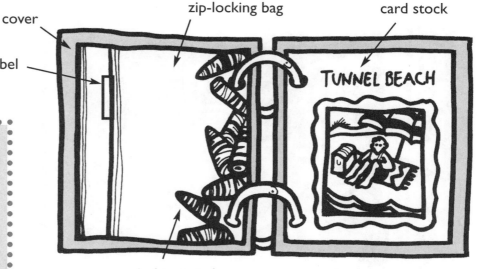

cover

label

zip-locking bag

card stock

TUNNEL BEACH

real objects in bags

label

THIS IS RALPH

Simple Spiral

Spiral-bound scrapbooks come in many sizes and are very affordable, so they're a quick (and cheap!) way to get started. Since spiral scrapbooks have a fixed number of pages, you can't add to them, but they're still fun to use and decorate with flat objects, like photographs and artwork. (Our family uses them for recording vacation memories en route.) Decorate the covers with stickers, die cuts, rubber stamps — even craft foam!

cut craft-foam frame to fit

cut craft-foam shapes

glue on foam frame and shapes

Hole-Punch Design

Making this cool-looking scrapbook is as easy as lacing up a shoe or tying a ribbon!

Let's do it!

1. Cut two identical pieces of poster board for the front and back covers.

2. Cut the card stock into pages ¼" (5 mm) smaller than the covers on all sides (so the edges won't show).

3. Cut two poster-board strips (use a different color) for the spine — each 1" (2.5 cm) wide and as long as the cover. Punch holes ½" (1 cm) in from the spine edge, leaving 1" (2.5 cm) between the holes. Cover with reinforcement circles. Use the punched spine as a template to punch holes in the covers and pages.

4. Decorate the pages; then, lace the scrapbook together with shoelaces or ribbon (see next page).

5. Decorate the cover. Color the reinforcement circles for more pizzazz.

reinforcement circles

punched holes

front cover

front spine

back spine

cut pages to fit inside covers

back cover

For easy lacing:

1. Start by leaving 7" (17.5 cm) at the top for tying a bow.

2. Bring the lace from around the back through each hole.

3. Bring the lace from around the back and cross over the first lacing.

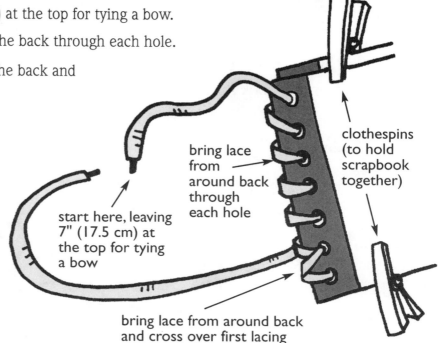

bring lace from around back through each hole

clothespins (to hold scrapbook together)

start here, leaving 7" (17.5 cm) at the top for tying a bow

bring lace from around back and cross over first lacing

Designer Lace-Ups

No colored shoelaces on hand? No problem! Use permanent markers to color and design your own!

Quick Starts Tips!™

A better bow. Want to make a pretty bow so both ends hang down (rather than going every which way)? Make your first part of the knot just as if you were tying your shoe, passing one lace over and under the other. Now, here's the trick:

1. Position the ends of the partially tied laces up and down (rather than left and right). Make a U-shaped loop in the bottom lace.

2. Bring the top lace down over the other lace and make a second loop. Tuck the second loop behind the first one and back up through the knot.

3. Tighten the ends. Your bow is perfect!

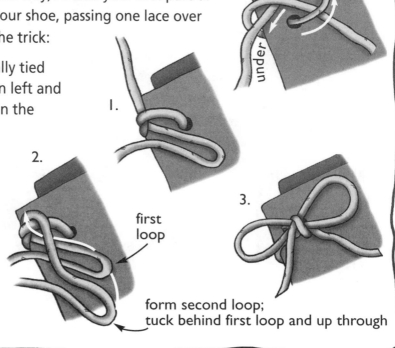

over

under

1.

2.

first loop

3.

form second loop; tuck behind first loop and up through

Make a Buddy Book

Give a scrapbook to a special friend or make a friendship memory book for yourself! Use the same instructions as for the HOLE-PUNCH DESIGN (pages 29–31), and include how you got to know each other and some of the funny things you've done together. Use ribbons for ties or hold the scrapbook together with paper fasteners. Add photos or artwork to the cover, then celebrate you and your friends inside!

ribbon ties

cut out cardboard flowers and glue over photos to "frame" them

Gift Rap

Include a message, poem, song, or rap around a matted photo on an inside page.

Lauren is your name, soccer is your game. You have long hair and you really like to share. You'll be my friend until the very end.

Pocket Surprise

Tuck a little gift into an envelope or pocket.

(see page 60 for heart pocket with flaps template)

Awesome Accordion Scrapbook

This simple connected-page scrapbook opens just like an accordion, with all the pages joined together. It works well for flat items like pressed flowers, leaves, photos, and artwork. Or, you can make an extra-special card, with photos on one side and a letter on the other. These are fun to make, fun to give, and fun to receive, too!

Materials

- *General supplies:* glue stick, scissors
- *Decorating supplies:* permanent markers, stickers, pens, paints, decorative paper
- Construction paper, 2 to 5 sheets
- Raffia, string, or ribbon

Let's do it!

1. Fold each piece of construction paper in half. Spread glue evenly on the *back side* of the first paper and press against the second paper. Press and smooth out any air bubbles. Continue gluing as many pages as you want.

2. Fold the accordian together and glue the raffia onto the back (you'll need enough to loop around the sides and tie in front).

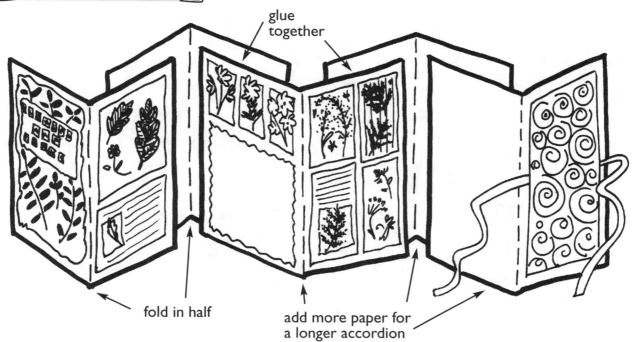

glue together

fold in half

add more paper for a longer accordion

3. Cut out decorative paper for the front and back covers; glue in place (the paper on the back cover goes over the raffia), pressing and smoothing out the paper.

4. Decorate the covers and inside pages.

FRONT COVER

BACK COVER

first glue raffia in place, then cover with decorative paper

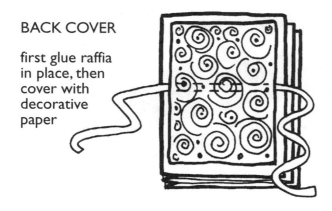

Wrap-Around Scrapbook

Use poster board, decorative papers, and souvenirs to make an almost-instant scrapbook for recording school trips or team events, Scout campouts, and family excursions. Along with the photos you took, add details about the fun things you did, and any new experiences or places you visited.

Materials

- *General supplies:* pencil, ruler, scissors, hole punch, glue stick
- *Decorating supplies:* colored pens, decorative papers, stickers, stamps, decals
- Poster board
- Card stock
- Paper fasteners

Let's do it!

1. Cut the poster board 8" x 11½" (20 x 28.5 cm) for the back cover and 8" x 10" (20 x 25 cm) for the front cover. Fold the back cover 1½" (3.5 cm) over the front to make the spine. (If you want a vertical book, vary the size of the covers, making sure the back cover overlaps the front by 1½"/3.5 cm on one side.)

2. Cut the card stock pages ¼" (5 mm) smaller than the front cover on all sides.

3. On the front cover, punch holes ½" (1 cm) from the top and sides and about 1½" (3.5 cm) apart. Use those holes as guides to punch holes in the back cover and card stock so that all the holes match.

4. Decorate the front cover, the folded-over spine, and the inside pages.

5. Assemble the scrapbook with paper fasteners.

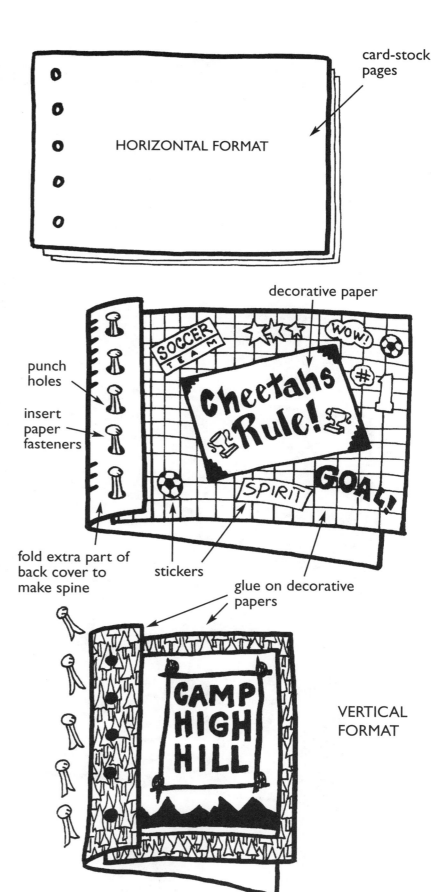

card-stock pages

HORIZONTAL FORMAT

decorative paper

punch holes

insert paper fasteners

fold extra part of back cover to make spine

stickers

glue on decorative papers

VERTICAL FORMAT

Sturdy Post-Bound Design

Post-bound scrapbooks lie flat, like a book, so they're good for nonbulky items such as photos and papers. The inside posts let you add or remove pages. A common size for store-bought post-bound scrapbooks is 12" x 12" (30 x 30 cm), but you can get them smaller or larger, and design the covers however you like (pages 41–57). Even better, make your own post-bound scrapbook from scratch, using paper fasteners!

Materials

- *General supplies:* ruler, scissors, hole punch, glue stick
- Heavy cardboard
- Self-adhesive paper
- Construction paper
- Card stock
- Paper fasteners

Let's do it!

To make the covers:

1. Cut two pieces of cardboard the same size. (A rectangular cover that measures 9" x 12"/22.5 x 30 cm holds 8½" x 11"/21 x 27.5 cm paper.)

2. Cut two 1" (2.5 cm)-wide strips of cardboard the same length as the *height* of the covers.

3. Lay one cover and strip on a sheet of self-adhesive paper (don't remove the backing yet), leaving ¼" (5 mm) between the pieces. Cut around the cardboard pieces, leaving about 3" (7.5 cm) extra on the left-hand side and 1" (2.5 cm) extra on the other sides.

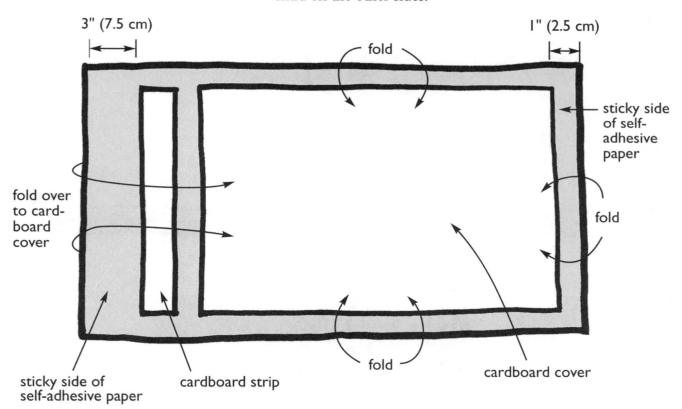

3" (7.5 cm)

1" (2.5 cm)

fold

sticky side of self-adhesive paper

fold

fold over to cardboard cover

fold

sticky side of self-adhesive paper

cardboard strip

cardboard cover

4. Remove the backing from the self-adhesive paper. Lay the cover piece and strip against the sticky side. Smooth out any air bubbles.

5. Fold the top and bottom of the self-adhesive paper to the inside; fold in the right side. Fold the left-hand edge over the cardboard strip so the edge is on the cardboard cover. Press firmly to smooth out any wrinkles.

6. Repeat steps 3 to 5 to make the back cover.

To complete and assemble:

1. Use the construction paper or self-adhesive paper to decorate the inside covers.

2. Punch holes on the inside strips, starting $1\frac{1}{2}$" (3.5 cm) in from the top and bottom with about 3" (7.5 cm) between holes.

3. Cut the card stock to fit; punch holes. Assemble the scrapbook with paper fasteners.

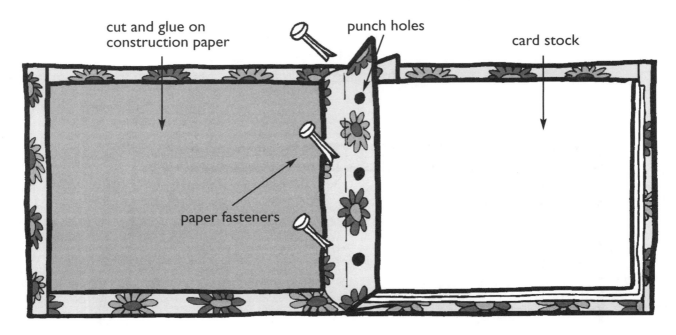

cut and glue on construction paper

punch holes

card stock

paper fasteners

Cool Covers

What's your style — bold and bright, soft pastels, lacy and delicate, or far-out and funky? You can buy scrapbooks in all sorts of colors and decorative designs, but to make your scrapbook reflect how very special the items inside it are, make your own cover design.

Add paper, quilted fabric, felt — even the seat of an old pair of denim jeans! — to turn any scrapbook into a masterpiece that's all your own! Pick a design that relates to your theme or choose your favorite colors and materials. Add stamped patterns, decoupage, gel-pen squiggles, and glued or sewn-on shapes.

Can't judge a book by its cover? Yes, you can — when you design that cover yourself!

Decoupage a Theme!

All it takes to transform the cover of any store-bought book is paper, cutout pictures, and glue. *Decoupage* (DAY-coo-pahj) is the art of cutting out pictures, gluing them in an arrangement on a flat surface, and then coating the design with a clear finish to protect it. You can use anything to make your decoupage design: magazine or catalog pictures and lettering, old postcards, greeting cards, gift wrap, maps, brochures, stationery, even photos and original works of art! If you can cut it out and glue it, you can decoupage it!

Let's do it!

1. Arrange the pictures on the cover until you have a design you like.

2. Working in sections (so that you can remember how you arranged the pictures), remove some of the pictures from the scrapbook and place them facedown. Choose your largest picture from that section. Using the paintbrush, lightly coat the back of the picture and the area on the cover where you want the picture to go with the diluted glue. Press the picture in place. Press out any air bubbles, gently wiping away excess glue with the paper towel. Now glue smaller pictures around the larger one.

3. Continue the same process, working in another section, until the design is complete. Let dry.

4. Brush the diluted glue mixture evenly over the entire design, covering all the edges and pictures. Let dry.

Quick Starts Tips!™

Special effects. Tickle your funny bone with a totally mixed-up photo. Draw body art, cut graphics from cards or other printed materials, or mix different photos to make a silly display!

start with a large background piece

glue on smaller or overlapping pieces

Cut on a tilt. While cutting, hold your scissors tilted slightly away from the paper. This creates an angled edge that will give your cut pieces a smooth, finished look.

Arrange it right. To get just the design you want, experiment with different arrangements. Overlap some pictures; leave space around others. Play around with letters and words, even your own name! Cut strips of solid or printed paper for a border.

Stamped stars, decorative writing, a snazzy border, a ticket stub, and an action photo — this cover has pizzazz!

Cut and print! Cut sponges into shapes to create unique textures and designs. Dip into paint; combine small shapes for borders and doodles.

Photo cutouts, silly card characters, fancy writing, and a simple border create a more subdued design.

Colorful Felt Design

Felt is the easiest fabric to work with because it has no "right" or "wrong" side (page 49) and the edges don't fray. Plus, felt is easy on your piggy bank — for under $5, you can buy enough to cover a large scrapbook! The bright colors are great for geometric designs, or you can trace and cut shapes from cookie cutters or templates. The directions given here are for a standard $10\frac{1}{2}$" x $11\frac{1}{2}$" (26 x 28.5 cm) three-ring binder, but feel free to use the same idea for other scrapbook sizes and styles, too.

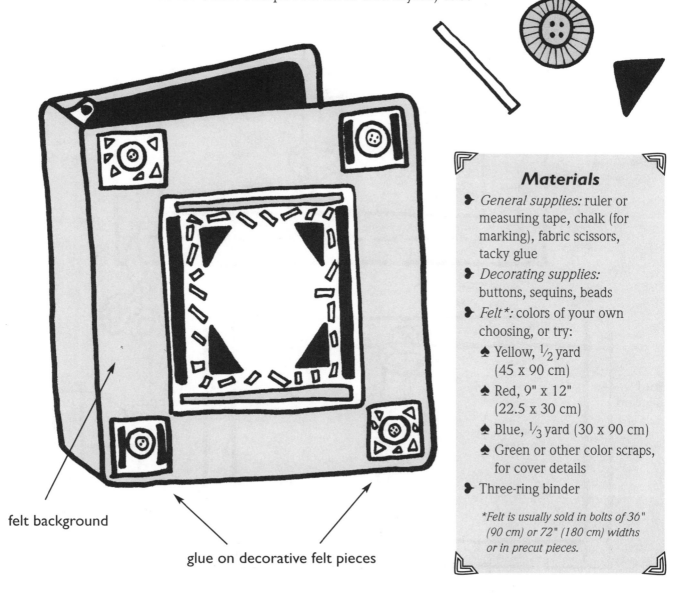

felt background

glue on decorative felt pieces

Materials

- *General supplies:* ruler or measuring tape, chalk (for marking), fabric scissors, tacky glue
- *Decorating supplies:* buttons, sequins, beads
- *Felt*:* colors of your own choosing, or try:
  - ♠ Yellow, $\frac{1}{2}$ yard (45 x 90 cm)
  - ♠ Red, 9" x 12" (22.5 x 30 cm)
  - ♠ Blue, $\frac{1}{3}$ yard (30 x 90 cm)
  - ♠ Green or other color scraps, for cover details
- Three-ring binder

*Felt is usually sold in bolts of 36" (90 cm) or 72" (180 cm) widths or in precut pieces.

Let's do it!

To cover the outside of the binder:

1. Place the open binder over the spread-out yellow felt. Mark a line on the felt 1" (2.5 cm) larger than the scrapbook on all sides; cut along line.

2. Glue the top and bottom edges in place, pulling the felt snug. Place dots of glue along the edges of the inside of the book. Pull the felt to the inside and press down.

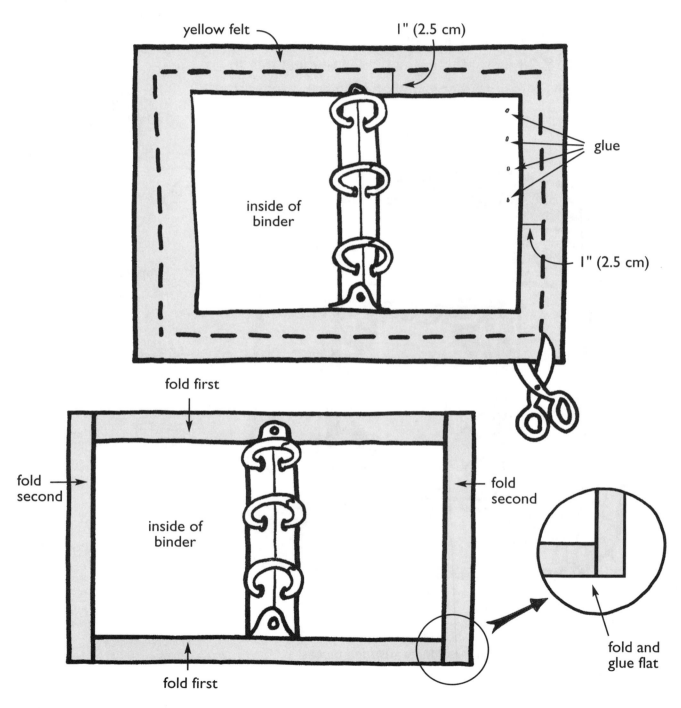

To cover the inside of the binder:

1. Cut two 2" x 12" (5 x 30 cm) strips of the red felt. Glue each one to the inside of the binder next to the rings, tucking one side of each felt piece under the rings. Weight down and let dry.

2. Cut two pieces of blue felt to fit inside each cover, hiding the other edges. Glue in place, weight, and let dry.

3. Glue a felt storage pocket to the inside cover.

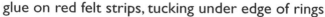

glue on red felt strips, tucking under edge of rings

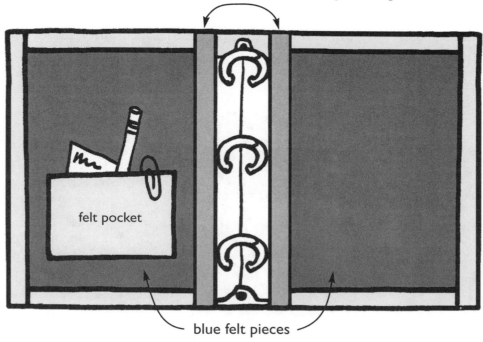

felt pocket

blue felt pieces

To finish:

Cut shapes and designs from the remaining felt to decorate the front. Sew or glue on buttons, sequins, and beads.

Quick Starts Tips!™

Make it stick! Because your scrapbooks are going to get a lot of use, it's important that the covers really hold together — and that means you need a good strong glue. I use tacky glue and place a book over the glued area while it dries.

Denim Cover with a Bandanna Sash

Denim makes a durable cover and the solid color is perfect for decorating, but if you prefer another color, these instructions will work with just about any fabric. Add stickers or contrasting fabric pieces, glue on your name with pipe cleaners, or stitch some words in yarn. Then, wrap on a bandanna sash for a finishing touch!

Materials

- *General supplies:* ruler or measuring tape, chalk (for marking), fabric scissors, tacky glue
- *Decorating supplies:* stickers, pipe cleaners, yarn, fabric scraps
- *Fabric:* prewashed denim, 1/2 yard (45 x 112 or 150 cm) or strips from old jeans, 15" (37.5 cm) wide
- Red felt or contrasting fabric, 1/3 yard (30 x 90 cm)
- Three-ring binder
- Red bandanna

Quick Starts Tips!™

Do it with denim. Denim is usually sold in bolts of 45" (112.5) or 60" (150 cm) widths. If you use felt for the inside covers, the smaller width is fine; if you want to use denim outside, choose the wider fabric.

Let's do it!

Follow the same steps that you use to make the COLORFUL FELT DESIGN (pages 45–47), with a few variations.

To cover the outside:

1. Lay the denim fabric *right side down* on a flat surface. Follow step 1, page 46, for cutting the fabric. If you plan on stitching your name on the cover, now's the time (see page 50).

2. Follow step 2, page 46, to glue the fabric.

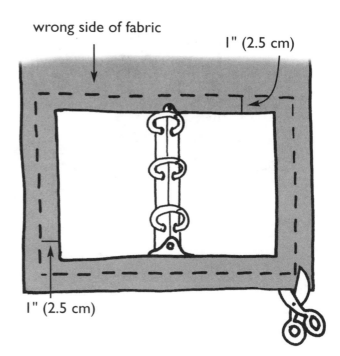

wrong side of fabric

1" (2.5 cm)

1" (2.5 cm)

Fabric: Right or Wrong?

Unlike felt, which is the same on both sides, most fabrics have a *right* and a *wrong* side. The right side is the finished material — the bright, printed side, or for denim, the "bluer" side. The wrong side is the faded side of the fabric, like the inside-out side of a shirt or dress. Marking is done on the wrong side of the fabric. And when you glue the fabric, you have to be sure that the wrong side of the fabric is against the glue, so that the right side will show!

To cover the inside:

Cut and glue two pieces of red felt to fit inside, covering the denim edges. (If you're using fabric rather than felt, cut the strips ½"/1 cm longer on all sides so you can fold under the cut edges.) Weight scrapbook and let dry.

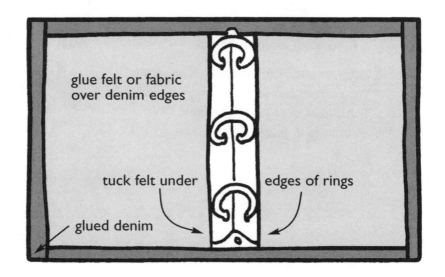

glue felt or fabric over denim edges

tuck felt under

edges of rings

glued denim

To finish:

Decorate the front with fabric scraps, stickers, and other items. Tie on the red bandanna sash.

Sew Your Name in Yarn!

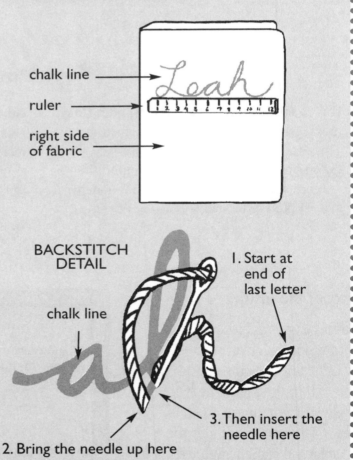

chalk line →

ruler →

right side of fabric →

After cutting the fabric to fit the outside of the binder (and before glueing it on!), gently tape the fabric, *right side up,* to the scrapbook, pulling slightly for a tight fit. Write your name in chalk on the front.

Remove the fabric and stitch your name in yarn over the chalk marks, using the back-stitch as shown below. Keep the yarn fairly loose — tight stitches will make the fabric buckle.

After you finished embroidering your name and any designs, continue covering the binder as in step 2, page 46.

BACKSTITCH DETAIL

chalk line

1. Start at end of last letter

2. Bring the needle up here

3. Then insert the needle here

Padded Fabric Cover

Make a padded cover using batting. Embellish it with ribbon or other trim for an old-fashioned look. For a fancy touch, add a MATCHING PADDED PHOTO FRAME (pages 53–54) on the front!

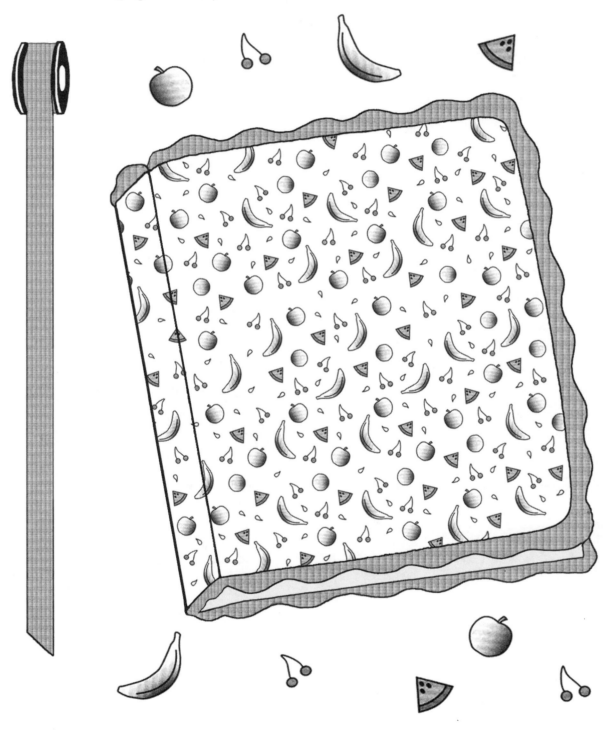

Quick Starts Tips!™

All about batting. This kind of batting has nothing to do with baseball. *Batting* is a fluffy material sold in various thicknesses called *lofts*. You can put it under your fabric to make your scrapbook softer and "cushiony." You can use batting, fiberfill (a loose type of stuffing), or even cotton balls for the padding.

Let's do it!

Follow the same basic steps as you used for the COLORFUL FELT DESIGN (pages 45–47), with a few additional steps.

To cover the outside:

1. Follow step 1, page 46 for cutting the fabric.

2. Cut a piece of batting the *same size* as the open binder. Glue it to the spine and then across the front and back. Weight scrapbook and let dry.

3. Follow step 2, page 46, for cutting and gluing the fabric.

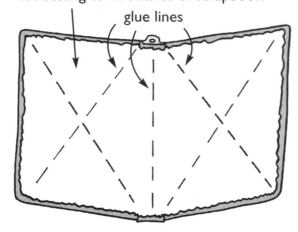

cut batting to fit outside of scrapbook

glue lines

To cover the inside:

Glue ribbon around the inside edges of the book. Cover the inside with fabric or felt, turning under the edges as needed. Weight scrapbook and let dry.

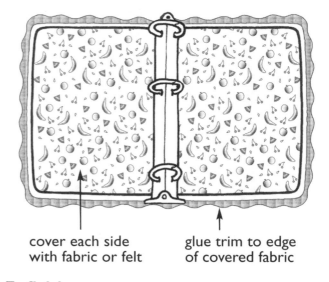

cover each side with fabric or felt

glue trim to edge of covered fabric

To finish:

Decorate the front with fabric pieces or a MATCHING PADDED PHOTO FRAME (pages 53–54).

Make a Matching Padded Photo Frame

Let's do it!

To make the cardboard frame:

1. Trace the photo onto the cardboard. Then remove the photo, and measure and mark two more lines: one *smaller* than your traced line, and another *larger*. Cut along the *outer and inner lines*.

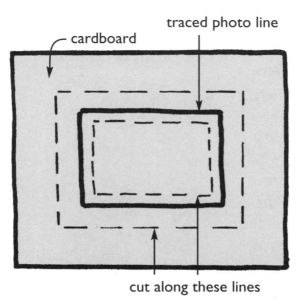

cardboard

traced photo line

cut along these lines

2. Glue cotton balls or batting on one side of the cardboard.

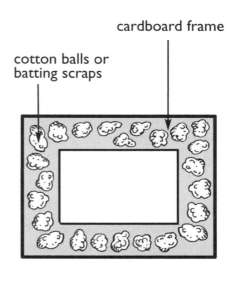

cardboard frame

cotton balls or batting scraps

Adding the fabric:

1. Center the cardboard frame onto the *wrong* side (page 49) of the fabric. Trace the inside edge. Snip a hole in the center of the fabric and cut an X to the corners.

2. Glue the cardboard frame, puffy side down, onto the wrong side of the fabric, matching it to the traced line. Fold the four inner fabric triangles to the back of the frame, and glue in place.

Then, fold in and glue down the outer corners and edges. Weight and let dry.

3. Decorate as desired.

To attach the frame to the scrapbook:

Glue the frame to the scrapbook cover, leaving the top unglued so you can slip a photo in or change your artwork.

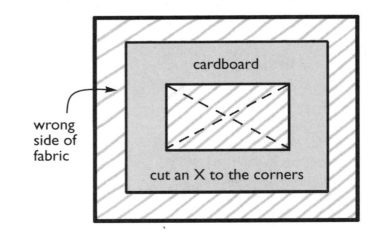

wrong side of fabric

cardboard

cut an X to the corners

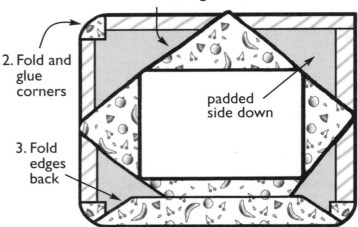

1. Glue fabric triangles to frame back

2. Fold and glue corners

3. Fold edges back

padded side down

Quick Starts Tips!™

Super-simple support! If you want to stand your frame up instead of attaching it to the front of your scrapbook, cut a piece of cardboard large enough to cover the back of the photo. Glue the piece of cardboard over the back of the photo, making sure the photo is lined up correctly in front. Then cut a wide strip of stiff cardboard about three-fourths the height of the frame. Fold over the top of the cardboard strip. Glue the bent portion in the middle of the cardboard piece. Adjust the angle of support, if necessary, so that the frame stands on its own.

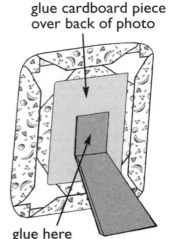

glue cardboard piece over back of photo

glue here

Decorated Canvas Cover

Let your scrapbook become a canvas for your next masterpiece! The tight, durable weave of canvas fabric is ideal for a scrapbook cover that you can bring to life with fabric paints, permanent markers, and stamped designs.

Quick Starts Tips!™

Testing, testing. Test all markers and inks on a scrap of canvas before using, to make sure they won't "bleed" (which could ruin your cover designs). Press the finished design with an iron (ask an adult for permission or help) to heat-set the colors.

As you like it! The directions on the next page explain how to cover a 12" x 12" (30 x 30 cm) post-bound book, but you can adapt the technique to a scrapbook of any size.

Materials

- *General supplies:* pencil, ruler or measuring tape, fabric scissors, tacky glue, craft scissors
- *Decorating supplies:* pens, markers, stamps and ink, fabric paints
- Post-bound album
- Canvas fabric, 2 yards (180 cm)
- Cereal-box cardboard

Acid Check

Any type of paper will work in a scrapbook, but acid-free papers are often preferred for long-lasting scrapbooks (see ARCHIVAL ALERT, page 12). To see if your papers are acid free, you can buy a special *pH tester pen* at craft stores. Just draw a small line on your paper (in an unnoticeable spot), and the line will change color to let you know the pH (acid level).

Let's do it!

To cover the outside:

1. Unscrew the inside posts to take the book apart. Lay the front cover on the canvas. Trace the edges. Measure and mark lines as shown. Cut along the outer line.

2. Apply glue to the top, bottom, and *inside* edges of the cover. Fold the canvas over the edges. Use scissors to poke holes. Press firmly. Glue the corners flat; weight and let dry.

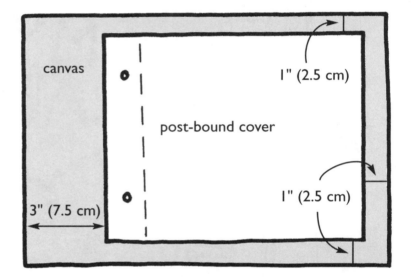

canvas

post-bound cover

1" (2.5 cm)

1" (2.5 cm)

3" (7.5 cm)

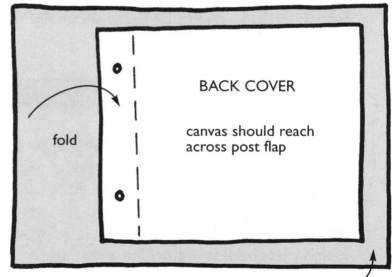

fold

BACK COVER

canvas should reach across post flap

fold and glue along inside edges and corners —

To cover the inside:

1. Cut pieces of cardboard to fit the inside front and back covers. Cut a piece of canvas to fit each piece of cardboard. Glue each piece of canvas to its matching piece of cardboard. Let dry.

2. Turn the covered cardboard over and glue to the inside cover, hiding the seams. Weight and let dry.

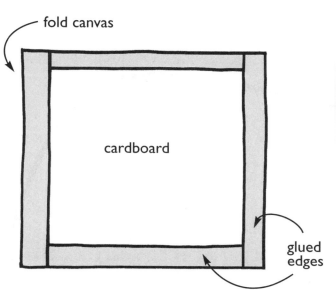

fold canvas

cardboard

glued edges

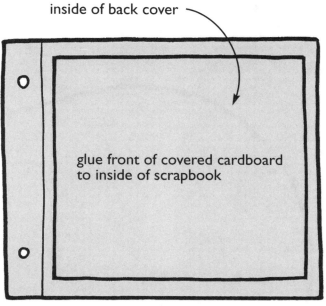

inside of back cover

glue front of covered cardboard to inside of scrapbook

To finish:

Repeat step 2 for the other cover. Reassemble the scrapbook with pages and decorate the blank canvas.

Quick Starts Tips!™

Sketch first ... All artists make sketches, so you should, too! On a piece of paper that's the same size as your "canvas," draw your design in pencil. Use a ruler to keep letters straight and evenly spaced. Adjust the sketch until you're satisfied with the result, then use colored pencils or markers to darken the design.

... then transfer. Carefully draw your design onto the canvas in pencil, using your sketch as a guide. Or, place graphite transfer paper on the front of the canvas, face down, and lay your sketch on top of it. Use the pencil to trace the design. Then remove the papers, and use fabric paints or fabric markers to color the sketch.

Templates

Apple Pocket

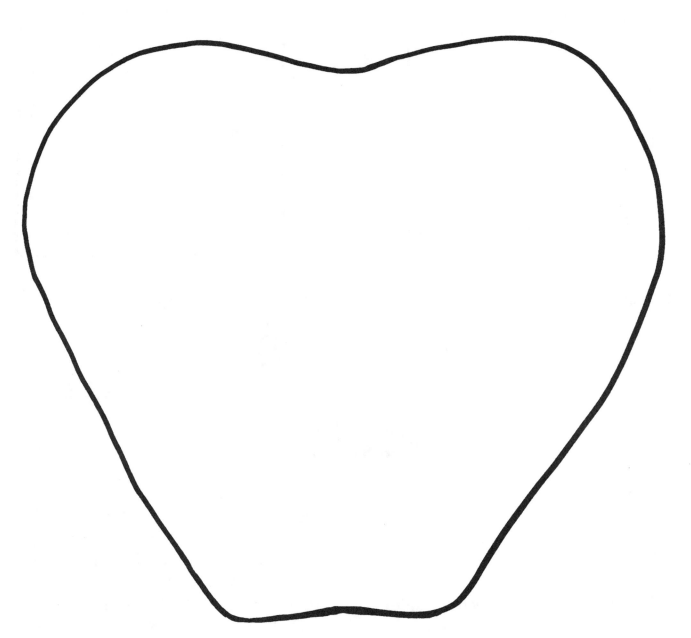

Heart Pocket

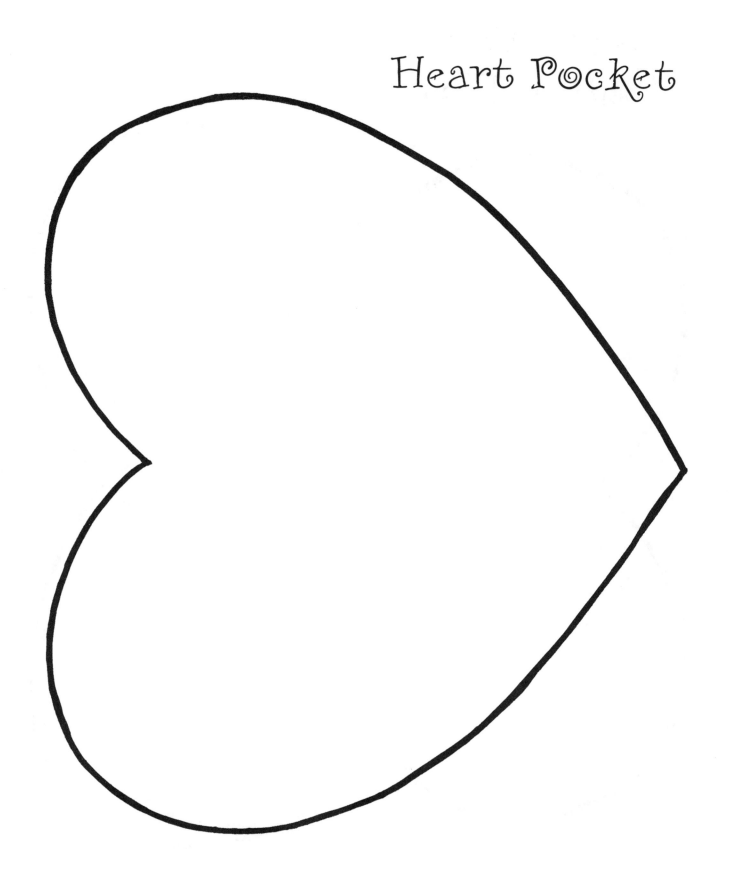

Heart Pocket
with Flaps

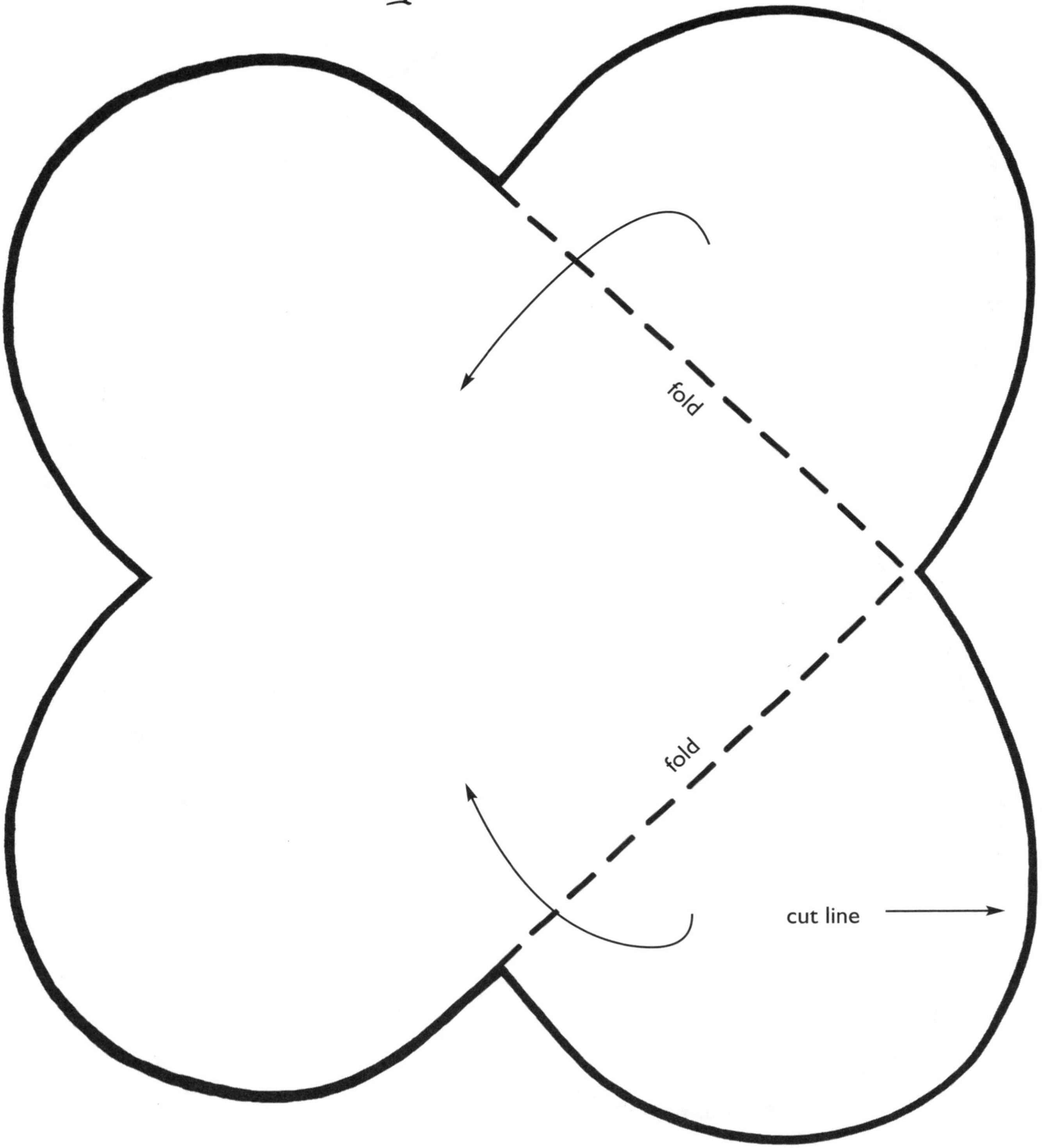

fold

fold

cut line

Gift Envelope

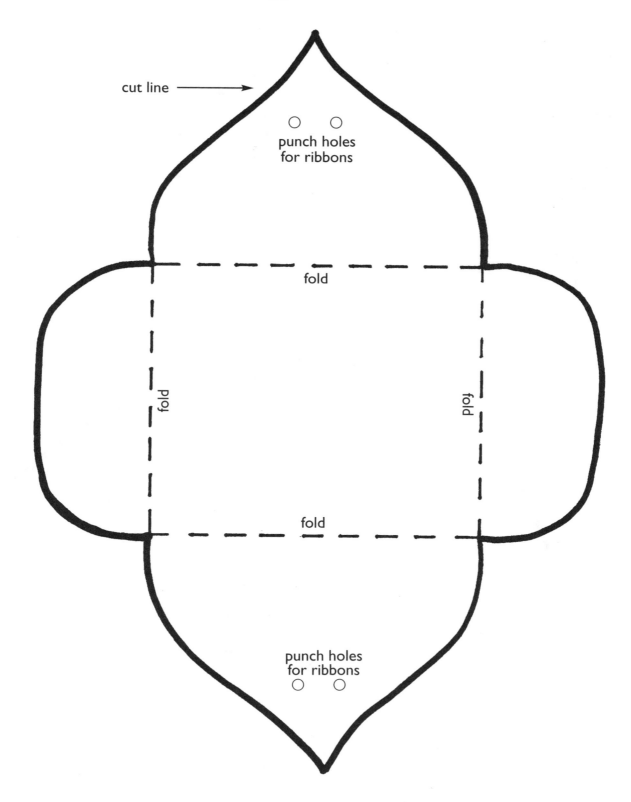

cut line →

punch holes
for ribbons

fold

fold

fold

fold

punch holes
for ribbons

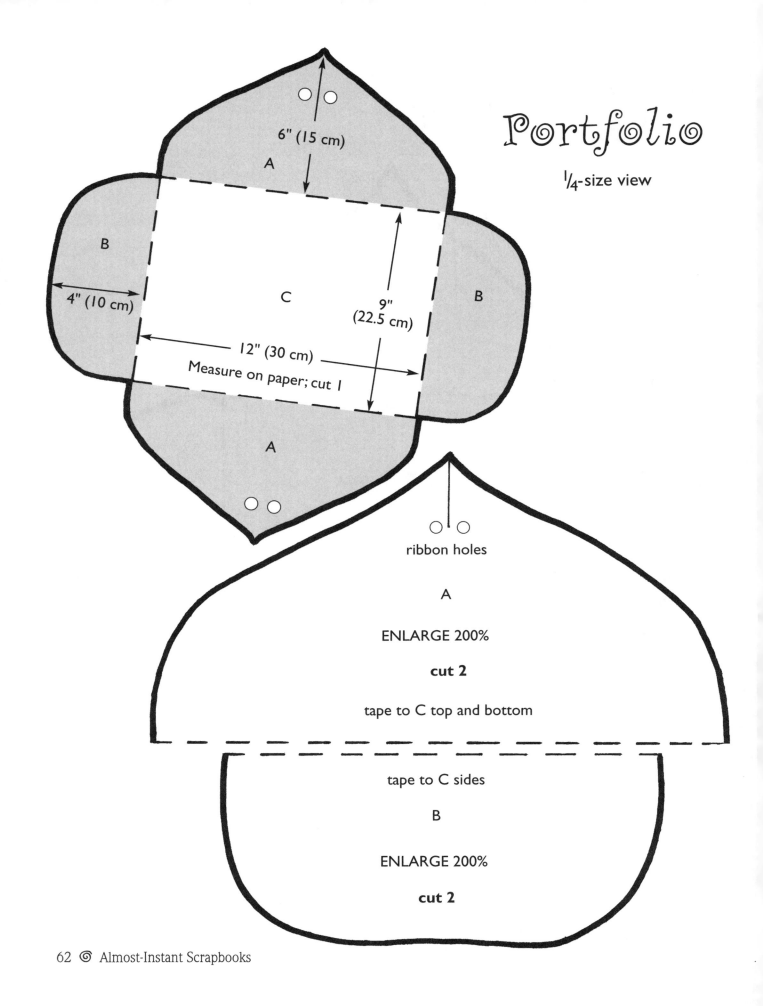

Portfolio

$1/4$-size view

6" (15 cm)

A

B

4" (10 cm)

C

9" (22.5 cm)

B

12" (30 cm)

Measure on paper; cut 1

A

ribbon holes

A

ENLARGE 200%

cut 2

tape to C top and bottom

tape to C sides

B

ENLARGE 200%

cut 2

Index

More Good Books from Williamson Publishing

Quick Starts for Kids!®

books for ages 8 to adult are each 64 pages, fully illustrated, trade paper, 8½ x 11, $8.95 US/$10.95 CAN.

REALLY COOL FELT CRAFTS
by Peg Blanchette & Terri Thibault

MAKE YOUR OWN FUN PICTURE FRAMES!
by Matt Phillips

KIDS' EASY KNITTING PROJECTS
by Peg Blanchette

KIDS' EASY QUILTING PROJECTS
by Terri Thibault

MAKE YOUR OWN HAIRWEAR
Beaded Barrettes, Clips, Dangles & Headbands
by Diane Baker

Parents' Choice Approved
BAKE THE BEST-EVER COOKIES!
by Sarah A. Williamson

GARDEN FUN!
Indoors & Out; In Pots & Small Spots
by Vicky Congdon

American Bookseller Pick of the Lists
MAKE YOUR OWN TEDDY BEARS & BEAR CLOTHES
by Sue Mahren

MAKE YOUR OWN CHRISTMAS ORNAMENTS
by Ginger Johnson

40 KNOTS TO KNOW
Hitches, Loops, Bends & Bindings
by Emily Stetson

Oppenheim Toy Portfolio Gold Award
DRAW YOUR OWN CARTOONS!
by Don Mayne

Dr. Toy 10 Best Socially Responsible Products
Dr. Toy 100 Best Children's Products
MAKE YOUR OWN BIRDHOUSES & FEEDERS
by Robyn Haus

KIDS' EASY BIKE CARE
Tune-Ups, Tools & Quick Fixes
by Steve Cole

MAKE MAGIC!
50 Tricks to Mystify & Amaze
by Ron Burgess

BE A CLOWN!
Techniques from a Real Clown
by Ron Burgess

YO-YO!
Tips & Tricks from a Pro
by Ron Burgess

DRAWING HORSES
(that look *real!*)
by Don Mayne

And More ...

Williamson's *Kids Can!*®

books for ages 7 to 14 are each 128 to 176 pages, fully illustrated, trade paper, 11 x 8½, $12.95 US/$19.95 CAN.

Parents' Choice Recommended
KIDS' ART WORKS!
Creating with Color, Design, Texture & More
by Sandi Henry

Benjamin Franklin Education/Teaching Gold Award
Parent's Guide to Children's Media Award
HAND-PRINT ANIMAL ART
by Carolyn Carreiro

Parents' Choice Gold Award
American Bookseller Pick of the Lists
THE KIDS' MULTICULTURAL ART BOOK
Art & Craft Experiences from Around the World
by Alexandra M. Terzian

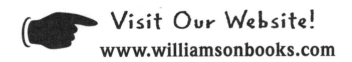

Visit Our Website!
www.williamsonbooks.com

To Order Books

We accept Visa and MasterCard (please include the number and expiration date). Order on our secure website or toll-free by phone with credit card:

1-800-234-8791

Or, send a check with your order to:

Williamson Publishing Company
P.O. Box 185
Charlotte, Vermont 05445

Catalog request: mail, phone, or e-mail <info@williamsonbooks.com>

Please add $4.00 for postage for one book plus $1.00 for each additional book. Satisfaction is guaranteed or full refund on books without questions or quibbles.